Fact Finders™

Biographies

Malcolm X

Force for Change

by Kristin Thoennes Keller

Consultant:
Dr. Kenneth Goings, Professor and Chair
Department of African American and African Studies
The Ohio State University
Columbus, Ohio

Capstone *press*

Mankato, Minnesota

Fact Finders is published by Capstone Press,
151 Good Counsel Drive, P.O. Box 669, Mankato, Minnesota 56002.
www.capstonepress.com

Library of Congress Cataloging-in-Publication Data
Thoennes Keller, Kristin.
    Malcolm X: Force for change / by Kristin Thoennes Keller.
    p. cm.—(Fact finders. Biographies)
    Includes bibliographical references and index.
    ISBN 0-7368-4347-7 (hardcover)
    1. X, Malcolm, 1925–1965. 2. Black Muslims—Biography—Juvenile literature. 3. African
Americans—Biography—Juvenile literature. I. Title. II. Series.
BP223.Z8L57784 2006
320.54'6'092—dc22   2004027199

Summary: An introduction to the life of civil rights leader Malcolm X.

Editorial Credits

Megan Schoeneberger and Roberta Basel, editors; Juliette Peters, set designer; Patrick D.
    Dentinger, book designer and illustrator; Kelly Garvin, photo researcher/photo editor

Photo Credits

AP/Wide World Photos/Angela Rowlings, 11; Eddie Adams, cover
Corbis/Bettmann, 1, 4–5, 8, 22, 24–25
Douglas County Historical Society Collections, 7
Getty Images Inc./Hulton Archives, 14, 15, 16–17, 18, 20–21, 23, 26; Time Life Pictures, 12,
    19, 27

1 2 3 4 5 6 10 09 08 07 06 05

Table of Contents

Chapter 1

Prison to Pride

In 1946, a 20-year-old African American man entered a prison in Boston, Massachusetts. He had been given a 10-year sentence for stealing. The man's name was Malcolm Little.

While in prison, Malcolm learned about a religion called the Nation of Islam, or the NOI. People who followed the NOI were called Black **Muslims.** Within a few years, Malcolm became a Black Muslim. Malcolm told many people about the NOI while he was in prison and after he was released.

Malcolm was a powerful speaker.

Malcolm became a famous speaker for the NOI. He spent the rest of his life teaching African Americans to be proud of who they are. Even after his death, people continue to love and respect Malcolm for his powerful message.

Chapter 2

A Hard Beginning

Malcolm Little was born May 19, 1925, in Omaha, Nebraska. He grew up during a difficult time for African Americans. White people often tried to hurt African Americans. Many **segregation** laws kept African Americans and whites apart.

Malcolm's parents were Earl and Louise Little. Earl was a Baptist minister and a human rights **activist**. He believed that African Americans should not try to be part of the white **society**. He said African Americans would never be treated as equals. Earl belonged to a group that thought African Americans should all return to Africa.

Omaha, Nebraska, where Malcolm was born, was a busy city.

In 1929, the Littles moved to Lansing, Michigan. They bought a house in an area where only white people lived. Their neighbors complained. When the Littles refused to move, angry men set fire to their house. It burned to the ground.

Classrooms were segregated during the time that Malcolm attended school.

When Malcolm was 6 years old, his father died. Earl was found dead after being hit by a **trolley**. It was clear that he had been beaten before the trolley hit him. Many people believed Earl was killed and then laid across the tracks. But his death was called an accident. Malcolm believed white men had killed his father.

Eight years later, Malcolm's mother was sent to a hospital for a mental illness. Malcolm and his brothers and sisters were split up. They were sent to different orphanages and foster homes.

Rising Anger

When Malcolm was in the eighth grade, he wanted to become a lawyer. His teacher told him an African American should choose a different job, such as a carpenter. Malcolm felt angry. He quit school.

Chapter 3

Trouble and Religion

In February 1941, Malcolm moved to Boston, Massachusetts. Over the next few years, he moved back and forth between Boston, New York City, and Michigan. Malcolm tried many jobs. He worked for a railroad company and as a waiter.

Trouble

Malcolm believed he was living in a world controlled by white people. He felt that a life of crime was his only choice. Malcolm began to use and sell drugs. He also started to steal. In 1945, Malcolm and some of his friends broke into houses and robbed them.

The Boston house where Malcolm lived is still standing today.

Prison Time

In January 1946, Malcolm was caught with a watch he had stolen. The police arrested him for stealing, carrying a gun, and breaking and entering. Malcolm was sentenced to 10 years in the Charlestown State Prison in Massachusetts.

Police took photographs of Malcolm after he was arrested in 1946. ▼

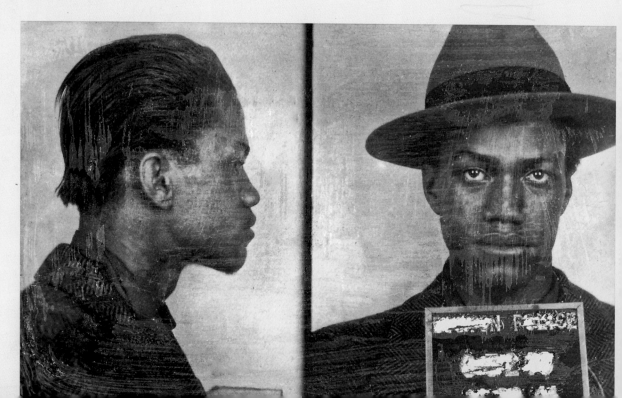

Malcolm's brothers visited and wrote to him in prison. They belonged to the Nation of Islam (NOI). They wanted him to become a Black Muslim like them.

The Nation of Islam

The NOI teachings made sense to Malcolm. Black Muslims worshipped Allah as God. They believed that African Americans were Allah's chosen people. They also believed that white people were evil. Malcolm agreed. He believed white people had caused his father's death and his mother's illness.

FACT!

Malcolm's nicknames were Big Red and Detroit Red because his skin looked reddish.

Malcolm did not know that the NOI was very different from traditional Islam. Islam teaches that all people are brothers and sisters, regardless of race.

In 1948, Malcolm began to write letters to Elijah Muhammad. Muhammad was the leader of the NOI. He wrote letters back to Malcolm. Soon, Malcolm joined the NOI.

Elijah Muhammad led the Nation of Islam until 1975. ▼

QUOTE

"I could spend the rest of my life reading, just satisfying my curiosity."
—Malcolm X

▲ Members
gathered for a
meeting of the
Nation of Islam
in the 1950s.

More Education

Malcolm used the prison library to teach himself. He read many books. He copied pages from the dictionary. After the lights were turned off at night, he read by the hallway light. Malcolm used his new knowledge to write letters for the NOI.

Chapter 4

A Powerful Speaker

In 1952, Malcolm was released from prison. The next year, he changed his name from Malcolm Little to Malcolm X. "Little" had been the name of the slave owner of his family. The X stood for his lost or forgotten African name. Black Muslims often used X as their last name.

Malcolm became a spokesperson for the NOI. He traveled to many cities to tell people about the NOI.

Malcolm was a powerful speaker. Wherever he went, African Americans gathered around him. The NOI membership grew from 500 to 30,000 while Malcolm was the spokesperson.

Malcolm visited college classrooms
to talk about the Nation of Islam.

The Civil Rights Movement

In the late 1950s, Malcolm's popularity grew. At the same time, the **civil rights** movement began. From 1955 to 1965, civil rights activists used nonviolent ways to make society equal for all people.

Malcolm disagreed with the activists. He did not want African Americans to join the white people. He wanted them to form their own society.

Malcolm believed African Americans should honor their African roots. ▼

Malcolm believed that whites would never allow equal rights. He said African Americans should fight back with violence.

Malcolm wanted African Americans to be in charge of their own futures. He encouraged them to start their own businesses.

Family

While Malcolm was working for the NOI, he met a Black Muslim named Betty X. Malcolm and Betty married in 1958. They had six daughters over the next seven years.

"Nobody can give you freedom. Nobody can give you equality or justice . . . You take it."

—Malcolm X

Malcolm had a close relationship with his daughters. ⬇

19

Chapter 5

A New Hope

In the early 1960s, Malcolm began to have doubts about the NOI. He and Elijah Muhammad disagreed about many things. In 1964, Malcolm left the NOI.

People Working Together

In April 1964, Malcolm visited the Islamic holy city of Mecca in Saudi Arabia. He joined the traditional Islam religion and changed his name to El-Hajj Malik El-Shabazz.

In Mecca, both light and dark Muslims treated Malcolm as a friend. He began to think that whites and African Americans could work together to end discrimination.

While traveling to Mecca, Malcolm met Prince Faisal al-Saud of Saudi Arabia.

↟ Malcolm (second from left) met with other Muslims while in Egypt.

After leaving Mecca, Malcolm went to Africa. He visited many countries, including Egypt, Nigeria, and Ghana. Malcolm met with leaders and spoke to many groups.

When Malcolm got home, he was hopeful. He was ready to work with other groups of people to help African Americans.

A New Group

In June 1964, Malcolm announced the beginning of a new group for African Americans. He called it the Organization of Afro-American Unity (OAAU). The group was for African Americans of all religions. It didn't matter if they were Christians or Muslims. Malcolm wanted all African Americans to work together.

By the 1960s, many people looked to Malcolm as a leader. He was liked by many people. Blacks and whites saw him as a voice for peace.

⬆ Malcolm gave speeches for the Organization of Afro-American Unity.

Chapter 6

A Life Cut Short

Although many people loved Malcolm, other people hated him. Many Black Muslims were angry at Malcolm. They believed he was not loyal to Elijah Muhammad. White racists also hated Malcolm. Malcolm was threatened many times. One time, his house was bombed.

On February 21, 1965, Malcolm was **assassinated** while speaking in New York City. He was shot 16 times. Later, three Black Muslims were arrested for the shooting.

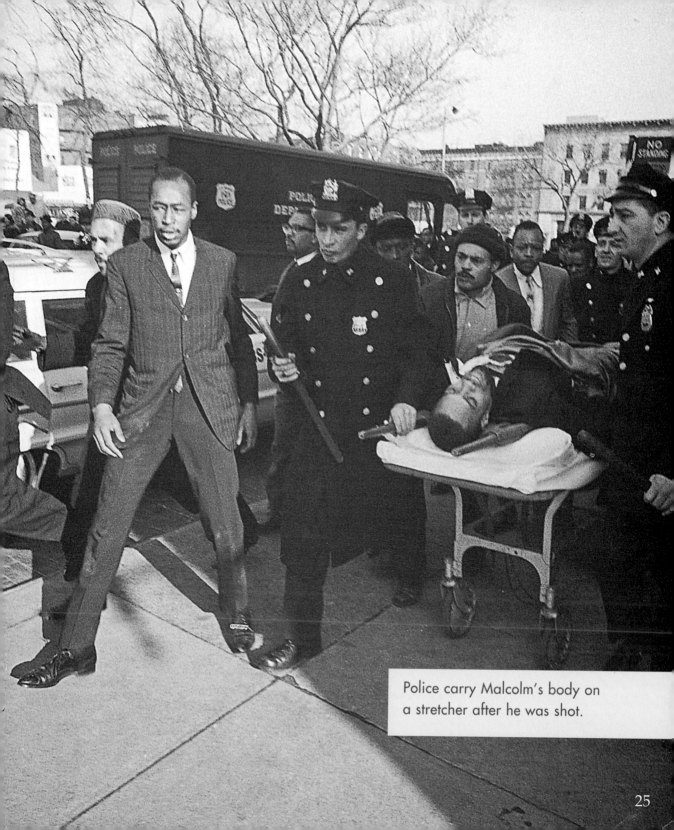

Police carry Malcolm's body on a stretcher after he was shot.

Lasting Message

Malcolm X encouraged African Americans to be proud of themselves. He told them not to let white people crush their spirit. Malcolm was a hero to many African Americans. Even today, people continue to be moved by Malcolm X.

▲ This portrait of Malcolm was taken a few months before he was killed.

QUOTE

"The future belongs to those who prepare for it today."

—Malcolm X

Fast Facts

Full names: Malcolm Little; Malcolm X; El-Hajj Malik El-Shabazz

Birth: May 19, 1925

Death: February 21, 1965

Hometown: Detroit, Michigan

Parents: Earl and Louise Little

Siblings: Ella, Mary, Earl Jr., Wilfred, Hilda, Philbert, Reginald, Wesley, Yvonne, Robert

Wife: Betty X

Daughters: Attallah, Qubilah, Ilyasah, Gamilah, Malaak, Malikah

Education: junior high school

Achievements:

Wrote *The Autobiography of Malcolm X* (with Alex Haley)

Convinced many African Americans to follow the Nation of Islam religion

Started the Organization of Afro-American Unity

Time Line

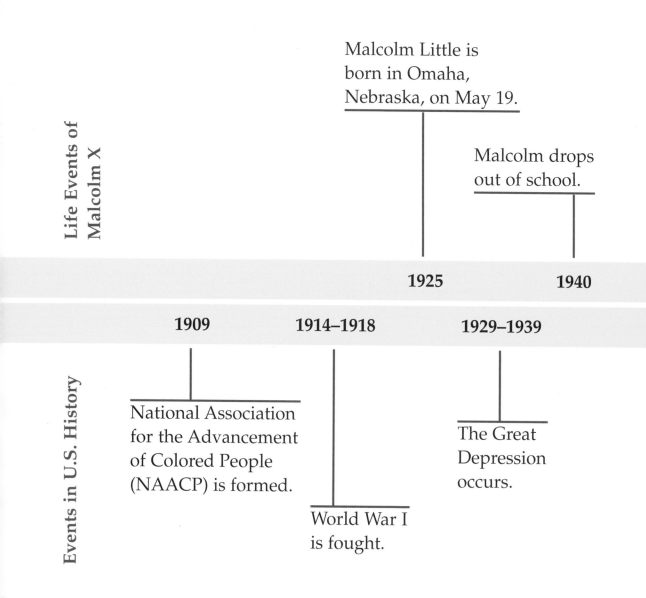

Life Events of Malcolm X

Malcolm Little is born in Omaha, Nebraska, on May 19.

Malcolm drops out of school.

1925

1940

1909

1914–1918

1929–1939

Events in U.S. History

National Association for the Advancement of Colored People (NAACP) is formed.

World War I is fought.

The Great Depression occurs.

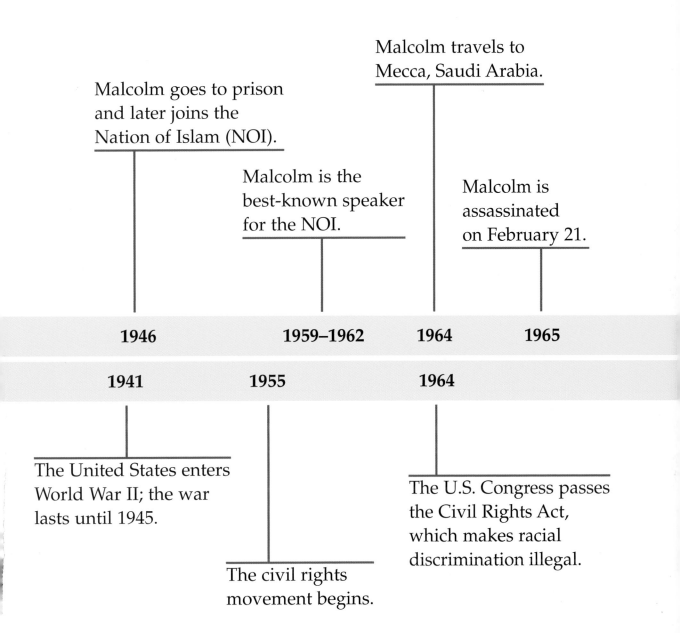

Malcolm goes to prison and later joins the Nation of Islam (NOI).

Malcolm travels to Mecca, Saudi Arabia.

Malcolm is the best-known speaker for the NOI.

Malcolm is assassinated on February 21.

1946 **1959–1962** **1964** **1965**

1941 **1955** **1964**

The United States enters World War II; the war lasts until 1945.

The U.S. Congress passes the Civil Rights Act, which makes racial discrimination illegal.

The civil rights movement begins.

Glossary

activist (AK-ti-vist)—a person who supports an important cause

assassinate (uh-SASS-uh-nate)—to murder someone who is well known

civil rights (SIV-il RITES)—the rights that all people have to freedom and equal treatment under the law

Muslim (MUHZ-luhm)—a person who follows the religion of Islam. Islam is based on the teachings of Muhammad.

segregation (seg-ruh-GAY-shuhn)—the act of keeping people or groups apart from one another

society (suh-SYE-uh-tee)—all people who live in the same country or area or share the same laws and customs

trolley (TROL-ee)—an electric street car that runs on tracks and gets power from an overhead wire

Internet Sites

FactHound offers a safe, fun way to find Internet sites related to this book. All of the sites on FactHound have been researched by our staff.

Here's how:

1. Visit *www.facthound.com*
2. Type in this special code **0736843477** for age-appropriate sites. Or enter a search word related to this book for a more general search.
3. Click on the **Fetch It** button.

FactHound will fetch the best sites for you!

Read More

Crushshon, Theresa. *Malcolm X.* Chanhassen, Minn.: The Child's World, 2002.

Draper, Allison Stark. *The Assassination of Malcolm X.* The Library of Political Assassinations. New York: Rosen, 2002.

Fitzgerald, Stephanie. *Struggling for Civil Rights.* On the Front Line. Chicago: Raintree, 2005.

Graves, Renee. *Malcolm X.* Cornerstones of Freedom. New York: Children's Press, 2003.

Index